Who Was

Susan B. Anthony?

D0051849

Who Was
Susan B. Anthony?

By Pam Pollack and Meg Belviso
Illustrated by Mike Lacey

Grosset & Dunlap
An Imprint of Penguin Group (USA) LLC

For Melina Reyes, Girl Power in full bloom—PP

For Smith College, Class of 1990—"Think your best
thoughts, speak your best word"—MB

GROSSET & DUNLAP
Published by the Penguin Group
Penguin Group (USA) LLC, 375 Hudson Street, New York, New York 10014, USA

USA | Canada | UK | Ireland | Australia | New Zealand | India | South Africa | China

penguin.com
A Penguin Random House Company

Library of Congress Cataloging-in-Publication Data is available.

ISBN 978-0-448-47963-7   10 9 8 7 6 5 4 3 2 1

Contents

Who Was
Susan B. Anthony?

November 5, 1872, was a presidential election
day. Ulysses S. Grant was running against
Horace Greeley. In Rochester, New York, men
sat by the ballot box to receive votes. The men of
Rochester entered the polling place, filled out a
ballot, and dropped it in the box. It was business
as usual.

However, in the doorway stood a middle-
aged woman in a black dress. Everyone
recognized her. It was Susan B. Anthony, the
greatest fighter for women's rights in the United
States. She had come with her three sisters. They
wanted to vote.

Women did not have the right to vote in
New York in 1872. Sometimes women filled out

ballots simply as a protest. These ballots were never counted. This year Susan decided to cast a vote herself. She had never done it before only because she spent so much time traveling the country giving speeches for voting rights that she was never at home long enough to prove she lived there—until that year.

Susan demanded a ballot. As a citizen of the United States, she said she had the right to vote. She had brought with her a copy of the Fourteenth Amendment of the Constitution, which guaranteed the right of citizens to vote. She had also brought a copy of the New York State Constitution.

The men felt that Susan was wrong. They believed that the Fourteenth Amendment gave only male citizens the right to vote. Susan looked them in the eyes. In her career she had faced down angry mobs; she'd been pelted with rotten eggs and tomatoes. Figures made to look like her had been dragged through the streets and burned—all because she wanted equal rights. These men were no match for Susan B. Anthony. They let her and her sisters vote.

Susan was thrilled.

But three weeks later as she sat in her parlor, there was a knock at the door. It was a deputy US marshall. He had come to arrest her. Susan held out her wrists to be handcuffed.

If the US government wanted a fight, she was ready.

Chapter 1
A Quaker Girl

Susan B. Anthony was the second oldest of seven children, five girls and two boys. She was born on February 15, 1820. Her father, Daniel, was a Quaker. Her mother, Lucy, had been a Baptist until her marriage. The Quakers didn't believe in dancing, singing, fancy clothes, or drinking, but they did believe that girls needed an education just like boys did. So Susan and her sisters Guelma, Hannah, and Mary would be educated along with her brothers Daniel and Jacob, called Merritt. (Her sister Eliza died when she was two years old.)

Susan lived in Adams, Massachusetts, until she was six. Then the family moved to Battenville where Susan's father opened a mill.

One day Susan came home from school upset. The boys in her class were learning long division. When Susan asked her teacher if she could learn it, too, he said that girls didn't need to learn long division.

So Daniel Anthony set up his own school at home where his daughters could get an equal education. Susan liked school. She also liked working at her father's mill whenever one of his employees got sick. She especially liked earning her own money—three dollars for two weeks of work! She used her salary to buy her mother six coffee cups and saucers.

But sometimes what happened at the mill puzzled Susan. One day she mentioned to her father that Sally Ann Hyatt, who was one of the workers, seemed to know more about weaving than her boss, Elijah. Why did Daniel not make *her* the boss? "It would never do to have a woman overseer at the mill," her father replied.

Susan accepted her father's word, but it didn't make sense to her. Why couldn't a woman be just as good a boss as a man?

In the evenings, after work and school were over, the family spent many happy hours together in the parlor. Daniel encouraged all his children to take an interest in the important issues of the day. One of these issues was temperance—the fight against making and drinking alcoholic beverages. Another was abolition, the fight against slavery.

When Susan was fifteen, she started to teach the younger children at her father's school. Two years later she traveled to the nearby town of Easton to live with a family and teach their children reading and writing. When the lessons were done, Susan helped with the household chores.

Daniel knew how much his daughter loved learning. He enrolled her in Deborah Moulson's Female Seminary in Hamilton, Pennsylvania. Susan was not very happy at the seminary. She missed her family.

Her time there was cut short by the Panic of 1837, an economic depression that wiped out many businesses in the United States, including Daniel's mill. Now the family had no money. All their possessions were put up for sale, including the cups and saucers Susan had given her mother.

Even their eyeglasses and underwear were sold!

Susan's father had always taught his children to be independent. Now it was time for Susan to show him what she had learned. She was going to earn her own living.

QUAKERS

THE QUAKERS, ALSO CALLED "FRIENDS," ARE A RELIGIOUS MOVEMENT. THEY BELIEVE THAT EVERY PERSON SHOULD FOLLOW THE "INNER LIGHT" OF GOD INSIDE THEMSELVES.

THE FIRST QUAKERS IN AMERICA CAME FROM ENGLAND IN THE SEVENTEENTH CENTURY. MANY CAME TO AMERICA TO FIND RELIGIOUS FREEDOM, THOUGH AT FIRST THE ONLY COLONIES THAT ACCEPTED QUAKERS WERE RHODE ISLAND AND PENNSYLVANIA. THEY WERE ORDINARY FARMERS WHO TRIED TO LIVE IN A WAY THAT BROUGHT THEM CLOSER TO GOD. THEY WORE SIMPLE CLOTHES AND DIDN'T TAKE PART IN PASTIMES LIKE DANCING, SINGING, OR DRINKING ALCOHOL.

IN THE UNITED STATES, THEY PLAYED A MAJOR ROLE IN THE FIGHT AGAINST SLAVERY. THE QUAKERS WERE ONE OF THE FIRST GROUPS TO PUBLICLY CONDEMN IT.

Chapter 2
The Smartest Woman in Canajoharie

Susan became an assistant teacher at Eunice Kenyon's Quaker boarding school in New Rochelle, New York. Teaching was one of the only jobs open to women at the time.

Susan was happy to find work. She was not so sure she liked the idea of marriage. After her sister Guelma's engagement to Aaron McLean, the son of a local judge, Susan never heard from her. There were no more letters. It was as if her sister had disappeared.

Susan wrote to Aaron with her fears. "I have no loved sister to whom I can freely open all my heart and . . . confide all my little griefs." Aaron's answer was not comforting: "Sisters are always twice as much trouble and bother as they are worth," he wrote.

For Aaron, this was just the normal joking of a man to his future sister-in-law. To Susan it wasn't funny. Once Guelma was married, she would no longer be allowed to own anything or enter into any contract on her own. Her husband would have the final word in every important decision in her life. According to the law at that time, a wife had no right to divorce her husband. Susan couldn't see how this was so different than being a slave.

Most women could not imagine any life other than being a wife and mother. When Susan's sister Hannah got married, Susan returned home to help with the wedding. Afterward, she took a new teaching job in Canajoharie, New York. Susan lived with her uncle Joshua and later her cousin Margaret. Susan and Margaret became great friends. Susan's father was now doing better, so she no longer had to send money home. She bought a white silk hat and a gray fox muff to keep her hands warm. She even went to her first dance. She was leaving some of her Quaker ideas behind.

But she had not abandoned the Quaker ideas about temperance and slavery. She was much more interested in these political movements than she was in teaching. She loved it when her father came to visit. The two of them argued about abolition with "the good old folks." That's what Susan called her relatives who still supported slavery. "The good old folks call us crazy fanatics now, the day will come when they must acknowledge their stupidity," she said.

On March 1, 1849, Susan gave her first public speech. It was to two hundred people at a supper for the Daughters of Temperance, an organization of women working for an end to the use of alcoholic beverages, such as wine, beer, and whiskey. Temperance was not just about banning alcohol. It was about helping

women married to drunkards. If a man spent the family money on alcohol or became violent, there was nothing a woman could do. Men were considered the head of the household. As such they had all the power, even if their children were in danger.

In her first speech, Susan made a special appeal to women. "Who are to urge on this vast work of reform? Shall it not be women, who are most aggrieved . . . ?" The next day it was said that, "Miss Anthony is the smartest woman who ever has been in Canajoharie."

Susan's happiness over her speech was followed by great sorrow when her cousin Margaret suddenly died after having a baby.

After Margaret's death, Susan returned home to her family's new house in Rochester, New York. It was often filled with her father's friends—political reformers, including Frederick Douglass, the ex-slave and great abolitionist.

While home in Rochester, Susan learned
about an unusual conference that had taken place
in Seneca Falls, New York, in July 1848. The
conference was for women's rights. The men and
women there argued for such shocking ideas as
greater legal rights for women, including women's

suffrage, which meant the right to vote. Women even got up to speak at the conference in front of men. That was completely unheard of at the time.

Susan had never thought about women fighting for their rights. Despite her Quaker education, she never thought about voting herself. She wanted to learn more about this women's rights convention.

FREDERICK DOUGLASS

FREDERICK DOUGLASS WAS BORN A SLAVE IN MARYLAND. HE LEARNED THE ALPHABET WITH SOME HELP FROM THE WIFE OF HIS OWNER AND LEARNED HOW TO READ ON HIS OWN. LATER HE SECRETLY TAUGHT OTHER SLAVES TO READ AS WELL. IN 1838, HE ESCAPED ON A TRAIN TO PHILADELPHIA DRESSED AS A SAILOR WITH FALSE PAPERS THAT SAID HE WAS FREE. AT AN ANTISLAVERY LECTURE, HE WAS ASKED TO STAND AND SPEAK. HE WAS SO GOOD AT IT THAT PEOPLE ENCOURAGED HIM TO BECOME A LEADER IN THE ABOLITIONIST MOVEMENT.

HE PUBLISHED HIS AUTOBIOGRAPHY IN 1845. IT BECAME A BEST SELLER, EVEN THOUGH SOME DOUBTED THAT A BLACK MAN COULD WRITE SO WELL.

IT'S STILL READ TODAY AS ONE OF THE BEST ACCOUNTS OF WHAT SLAVERY WAS REALLY LIKE. DOUGLASS WAS THE ONLY AFRICAN AMERICAN TO ATTEND THE FIRST WOMEN'S RIGHTS CONVENTION IN SENECA FALLS IN 1848.

Chapter 3
New Friends

In 1850, Susan started working with the Underground Railroad in Rochester. The Underground Railroad was a network of people who helped smuggle slaves from the south to free states in the north. That year, she attended an antislavery meeting in Syracuse, New York. The slavery question was now debated everywhere. The 1850 Fugitive Slave Law said that a slave owner who found an escaped slave could capture

him again, even if the slave was in a free state. At the meeting, Susan listened to prominent abolitionists like William Lloyd Garrison and George Thompson.

WILLIAM LLOYD GARRISON

BORN IN 1805, WILLIAM LLOYD GARRISON GREW UP THE SON OF A SINGLE MOTHER AFTER HIS FATHER ABANDONED THE FAMILY. AS A BOY, HE WAS AN APPRENTICE AT THE *NEWBURYPORT HERALD* NEWSPAPER. LATER HE BECAME A PUBLISHER WHO TRAVELED THE COUNTRY SPEAKING OUT AGAINST SLAVERY. HE FOUNDED THE NEW ENGLAND ANTISLAVERY SOCIETY AS WELL AS HIS OWN ANTISLAVERY NEWSPAPER CALLED *THE*

LIBERATOR. AFTER THE CIVIL WAR, WHEN SLAVERY WAS FINALLY ABOLISHED, HE CONTINUED TO WRITE AND LECTURE IN SUPPORT OF CIVIL RIGHTS FOR WOMEN AND BLACK PEOPLE. HE DIED IN 1879.

After the meeting, Susan's friend Amelia Bloomer, who edited an abolitionist newspaper called *The Lily*, invited her to Seneca Falls. One day on the street, Amelia introduced Susan to a friend of hers, Elizabeth Cady Stanton. Elizabeth was one of the women who had organized the women's rights convention. Elizabeth didn't have much time to talk that day—Garrison and Thompson were staying at her house and she was worried what her three small sons might get up to while she was gone. But even in those few minutes, the two women made a lasting impression on each other. Elizabeth's clothing also made an impression. She and Amelia both wore skirts that ended just below the knee over pants. This new style would come to be called "Bloomers," after Amelia— and it was shocking.

A few months later in January 1852, Elizabeth went to a meeting for the Sons of

Temperance in Albany. She took her seat with the other ladies of the Daughters of Temperance. After listening to the men talk for a while,

Susan stood up to speak, too. She was immediately told that "the sisters were not invited to speak, but to listen and learn."

Susan was so angry that she marched out of the hall. She told her new friend Elizabeth Cady

Stanton about what happened. Elizabeth agreed with her that they should start their own group. Susan founded the Women's New York State Temperance Society, with Elizabeth as president. When Elizabeth came to speak, not only was she wearing bloomers, but she'd bobbed (cut short) her hair!

Elizabeth had great influence on Susan. Susan began to see that without rights, women could not affect the laws of the land. Susan began to argue for women to have the right to vote. She started wearing bloomers, too. In June of 1853, she and Elizabeth celebrated the one-year anniversary of the temperance society they had started. Elizabeth made a speech about women's rights, including divorce rights.

After the speech, the society took a vote on whether or not to allow men to hold offices within their temperance society. Elizabeth and Susan supported the idea. They thought men and women could work together. After all, the changes they wanted to make for women would be good for all of society. The men were given the right to hold office.

Almost immediately, the men present, with the help of many of the women, voted Elizabeth out as president. They changed their name to the Peoples' League and rejected any support of women's rights!

Susan was furious. She couldn't believe a society she created would not support women's rights! Elizabeth cheered her up. "Now Susan," she said, "I do beg of you to let the past be the past. . . . We have other and bigger fish to fry."

Chapter 4
I Will Stand by You

On December 25, 1854, Susan left her home in Rochester to go on a statewide lecture tour. She planned to visit every single one of New York's fifty-four counties in four months. She spoke in favor of the right for married women to own property. She was no longer wearing bloomers.

Sometimes she had been surrounded by jeering crowds just for wearing them. Elizabeth convinced her to stop.

Traveling through New York State in the dead of winter was not easy. Along the journey, she met a Quaker man who offered to drive her in his fine sleigh. He heated logs to warm her feet while they traveled and waited for her outside of her meetings.

Elizabeth was glad for the comfort—until it turned out the man wanted to marry her! Not only did he want her to give up her life's work, he believed he was rescuing her from the "terrible fate" of being an old maid! (In the 1850s, most people thought that there was nothing worse than being a single woman, an "old maid"!) Susan turned down his marriage proposal.

Susan's punishing schedule gave her terrible back pain, but she continued on. She kept careful accounts of all the money she spent. Her only salary came from the twenty-five-cent fee people paid to hear her speak.

While traveling around New York, Susan visited her married sisters Guelma and Hannah. Her sisters were proud of the work she was doing. When Susan visited them, she knew that a life as a wife and mother was not for her. She also returned to speak in Canajoharie. She saw a lot of old friends, including her uncle Joshua.

When the staff of her old school tried to get her to return as a teacher, her uncle said, "No!" Anyone could teach, her uncle said, but Susan's real calling was "to go around and set people thinking about the laws."

She returned home for a rest with her family. Her sister Mary was now a teacher. Her brother Merritt talked about his plans to move out to Kansas to join the abolitionist leader John Brown.

Susan began work for the Anti-Slavery Society. She brought her opinions on women's rights and abolition to teacher's conferences as well. In 1857, she shocked the New York State's teacher's

convention by demanding that black and white children attend the same schools. Those schools, Susan said, should also be coed. That meant both boys and girls could attend.

In 1860, Susan and Elizabeth scored a major victory. Thanks to their efforts, New York State granted married women the right to own property and carry on business in their own names. By the time Abraham Lincoln was elected president in 1861,

PRESIDENT ABRAHAM LINCOLN

Susan was hard at work for the abolitionist movement. At that time, even though Lincoln was personally against slavery, he still defended the rights of slave owners. He promised to stop the spread of slavery rather than get rid of it. Susan would accept nothing less than the end of slavery and equal rights for African Americans.

She put together an abolitionist lecture tour with Elizabeth. Angry mobs of boys and men met them at every station, booing, hissing, and throwing rotten eggs. Figures made to look like Susan were dragged through the streets and burned in the public square. In Utica, New York,

a mob prevented Susan from entering the hall where she was to speak against slavery. The mayor offered to "escort" her to safety. "I am not afraid," said Susan. "It is you who are the coward . . . I scorn your assistance." The mayor dragged her away from the hall by force.

The Civil War began on April 12, 1861. With the country at war, Elizabeth thought they should put the fight for women's rights on hold. Susan disagreed, but went along with Elizabeth. They would both come to regret that decision.

Chapter 5
Betrayal

Elizabeth believed that if women worked hard for the war effort, they would be rewarded with voting rights when the union was saved. Susan was not so sure. On April 10, 1862, she was proved right. The New York State legislature, no longer pressured by the women's rights movement, put a stop to many parts of a law that gave married women the right to own property and do business. This was the same law that women had won just two years earlier. "Well, well," Susan wrote, "while the old guard sleeps the young 'devils' are wide-awake." To Susan this was a lesson: If she stopped fighting even for a minute, she would lose things for which she had fought.

Despite her disappointment in the fight for women's rights, Susan continued to speak against slavery. In early November, she returned to Rochester for a visit. One Sunday morning, Susan and her father, Daniel, were talking about Abraham Lincoln's recent Emancipation Proclamation. The proclamation freed all the

slaves in the southern states. Daniel suddenly got a terrible stomachache. Susan helped him to bed. But, sadly, he did not recover and died two weeks later. His funeral was attended by many famous abolitionists, including Frederick Douglass.

Susan was stunned by her father's death. He had always been one of her greatest supporters. She hated to think of her mother and her sister Mary living all alone without him. But she knew her father would want her to continue her work. She and Elizabeth arranged a women's meeting in New York City. The women there fought for universal suffrage. That meant the right to vote for all people—black and white, men and women.

With the end of the Civil War in April 1865, suffrage became an even more important question. A new amendment to the Constitution was proposed in Congress. The amendment would give black people the vote. It called for all citizens to have the right to vote, but defined *citizen* as *male*. For the first time, the wording of the Constitution was being changed to intentionally leave out women.

Susan was furious. The abolitionists had taken a good idea—votes for black people—and attached it to a bad idea—no votes for women. At a meeting of the Anti-Slavery Society in 1866, president Wendell Phillips declared it the "Negro's hour." He thought it was selfish of women to interfere with black suffrage by asking for it for themselves. Elizabeth Cady Stanton snapped, "Do you believe the African race is composed entirely of males?"

Susan and Elizabeth presented Congress with a petition for women's suffrage with ten thousand signatures, but abolitionists stuck to their male-only stance. The New York State Congress removed the word *white* from its own definition of citizen but not the word *male*. The Anti-Slavery Society turned its back on Susan. They wouldn't even print her letters in their newspaper. "The gate is shut, wholly," Susan said.

The abolitionists accused women of trying to keep black people getting the right to vote by demanding that women get their rights at the same time. Black women had not yet gotten much of a chance to organize themselves to ask for suffrage. But one black woman spoke out on the subject. Sojourner Truth said, ". . . there is a great stir about colored men getting their rights but not a word about the colored women theirs. You see, the colored men will be the masters over the women."

SOJOURNER TRUTH

SOJOURNER TRUTH WAS BORN ISABELLA BAUMFREE IN 1797. SHE WAS BORN INTO SLAVERY IN SWARTEKILL, NEW YORK. SHE RENAMED HERSELF SOJOURNER TRUTH AFTER ESCAPING SLAVERY WITH HER INFANT DAUGHTER, SOPHIA. LATER SHE LEARNED THAT HER SON PETER WAS BEING ABUSED BY HIS MASTER. SHE THEN BECAME THE FIRST BLACK WOMAN TO CHALLENGE A WHITE MAN IN COURT AND WIN. AT A WOMEN'S RIGHTS CONVENTION IN OHIO, SOJOURNER DELIVERED A FAMOUS SPEECH CALLED "AIN'T I A WOMAN?":

FREE LECTURE!
SOJOURNER TRUTH.

"I COULD WORK AS MUCH AND EAT AS MUCH AS A MAN—WHEN I COULD GET IT—AND BEAR THE LASH AS WELL! AND AIN'T I A WOMAN?"

DURING THE CIVIL WAR, SOJOURNER HELPED RECRUIT BLACK TROOPS FOR THE UNION. IN 1864, SHE MET ABRAHAM LINCOLN.

SHE FAMOUSLY RODE HORSE-DRAWN STREETCARS IN WASHINGTON, DC, TO SHOW THAT BLACK PASSENGERS SHOULD BE ALLOWED TO SIT NEXT TO WHITES—AND SUCCEEDED. SHE DIED IN 1883.

Susan and her friends found a new enemy in Horace Greeley, the editor of the *New York Tribune*. The *Tribune* was one of the most important newspapers in the country. Greeley had once supported women's rights. Now he sided with the male-only abolitionists. He filled his newspaper with arguments against the woman's vote. "The best women I know do not want to vote," he claimed. He banned all press about Susan. If forced to write about Elizabeth in the society pages, he vowed

HORACE GREELEY

only to refer to her as Mrs. Henry B. Stanton. In other words, he would describe her by naming the man to whom she was married. He would never mention any of her own accomplishments.

Susan and Elizabeth realized that if women were going to get equal rights, they would have to fight for it themselves.

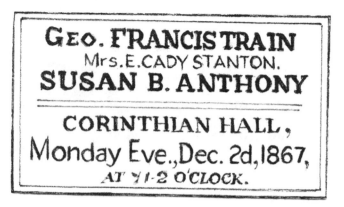

GEO. FRANCIS TRAIN
Mrs. E. CADY STANTON.
SUSAN B. ANTHONY

CORINTHIAN HALL,
Monday Eve., Dec. 2d, 1867,
AT 7 1-2 O'CLOCK.

Chapter 6
The *Revolution*

Susan traveled to Kansas to speak for women's rights. She was joined by George Francis Train. Train had been sent by Henry Blackwell, the husband of Lucy Stone, another women's rights activist who worked with Susan. Train was a Democrat. He supported women's

GEORGE FRANCIS TRAIN

suffrage, but he was also a Copperhead. That meant that he was pro-slavery. Although Susan disagreed with his stance on slavery, Train was a good speaker on women's rights.

Train announced that he would fund a women's rights newspaper. The *Revolution* would be a weekly paper. Its motto: "Men, their rights, and nothing more; women their rights, and nothing less." Susan managed the paper. Elizabeth Cady Stanton and Parker Pillsbury were the editors.

Republicans— the antislavery party—condemned the whole thing.

Horace Greeley refused to print an announcement of the paper in the *Tribune*. The editor of the *New York Sunday Times* said that Elizabeth should tend to her "domestic duties" and Susan needed "a good husband and a pretty baby."

The first issue appeared on January 8, 1868. The paper was open to all sorts of subjects, even those considered forbidden elsewhere. In it, Elizabeth argued for better divorce laws, equal pay for women, and the right for women to wear pants.

In February 1869, Republicans in Congress proposed a new amendment to protect voting rights. It said that the right to vote should not be denied on account of "race, color, or condition of previous servitude."

"Or sex!" Susan and her friends wanted to hear.

But Republicans refused to include women. Susan could not support the proposed amendment as long as it excluded women.

Susan and Elizabeth called a women's meeting in New York where they formed a new organization: the National Woman Suffrage Association. They used the term "National" because they were fighting for an amendment to the US Constitution that gave women the right to vote in every state.

NATIONAL
WOMAN
SUFFRAGE
ASSOCIATION
NWSA

Meanwhile, at a conference in Cleveland, Lucy Stone and others created the American Woman Suffrage Association. "The American" group called for suffrage on a state-by-state basis instead of a national amendment.

AMERICAN
WOMAN
SUFFRAGE
ASSOCIATION

They said it was not meant to go against the National group, but everyone involved saw the split in the movement. The members of the American group were richer and followed the rules of polite society more than Susan's group.

Susan and Elizabeth were still printing the *Revolution*, but they were losing money fast. Elizabeth's shocking ideas drove advertisers away. Another suffrage activist, Isabella Hooker, asked her half-sister Harriet Beecher Stowe, who was a famous author, to publish her new book in the *Revolution* in segments. That would be sure to bring in advertisers. But Isabella's half-sister had a condition—the paper needed to change its name to something nicer. Susan asked Elizabeth what she thought. "My dear Susan," said Elizabeth, ". . . I consider it a great mistake. A journal called *The Rosebud* might answer for those who come with kid gloves and perfumes . . . but for us . . . there is no name like the *Revolution*."

The author withdrew her offer. The *Revolution* closed down in May of 1870 with a debt of $10,000. Susan set out on a lecture tour to pay it off.

Chapter 7
Been and Gone and Done It

The split between the
National and the American
women's suffrage groups was
still bitter. The American,
unlike the National, allowed
men to hold office. Henry
Ward Beecher was its
first president. He tried
to get all women's
suffrage organizations

HENRY WARD BEECHER

to become part of the American.

By this time, Susan was almost fifty. She
was becoming a legend in the United States.
The press called her Napoleon (after the
French emperor who conquered most of Europe),

Bismark (after the politician who made Germany a strong power), and The General. At her birthday party that year, she stood up to speak to a group of her friends who had gathered to celebrate. She was tongue-tied. She explained, "If this were an assembled mob opposing the rights of women I should know what to say." At this point in her life, Susan was more prepared to speak to complete strangers on women's suffrage than to her own dear friends.

Susan went home to Rochester just in time to vote in the national election of 1872. By voting, Susan was declaring that she believed she ought to have the right to vote. Her sisters Guelma, Mary, and Hannah went with her. Afterward she wrote to Elizabeth, "Well, I have been & gone & done it!! Positively voted the Republican ticket—straight—this AM at seven o'clock & swore my vote in at that."

Three weeks later, Susan was arrested for her vote. She was offered bail. That meant she could pay money as a promise that she would not run away before her trial. Susan refused to pay. But her lawyer, Henry Selden, couldn't bear to see a lady he respected in jail. Even though his actions interfered with what Susan was trying to do, Selden paid the bail money to get Susan out of jail.

Susan's trial began June 17, 1873. The judge was Associate Justice Ward Hunt. Hunt believed that Susan was not smart enough to speak for herself because she was a woman. Selden argued for her. When they were finished, Judge Hunt pulled a piece of paper from his pocket. It was his decision. He had written it before he had even listened to what Susan's lawyer had to say. Hunt told the jury to find Susan guilty. When Selden tried to ask the jurors what they thought, Hunt sent the jury away without a verdict. "Has the prisoner anything to say why sentence shall not be pronounced?" he asked.

Susan rose from her chair. "I have many things to say," she began.

"You have trampled underfoot every vital principle of our government." The judge tried to silence Susan, but she would not be quiet. When she finally finished her accusations, the judge ordered her to pay a hundred-dollar fine. "I will never pay a dollar of your unjust penalty," Susan declared. She promised to continue to "rebel against your man-made, unjust, unconstitutional forms of law that tax, fine, imprison, and hang women, while they deny them the representation in the government. . . . Resistance to tyranny is obedience to God."

"Madam," the judge replied, "the Court will not order you committed until the fine is paid."

This made no sense! The judge was telling Susan that unless she paid her fine, he would *not* put her in jail. Judge Hunt knew that if he didn't put Susan in jail, she could not ask another court to look at his decision. In this way, he kept her from taking her case to a more important court. That's what Susan wanted to do. Instead, the judge closed the case. Susan never paid a fine or went to jail. She also didn't get to fight in a higher court for the right to vote.

Susan's trial had put the question of women's suffrage on the front page. That was a victory. But Susan could not enjoy it.

THE DAILY GRAPHIC

Her sister Guelma became sick with tuberculosis. Susan, Hannah, and Mary cared for her together until she died.

Susan was in no mood to travel. But the *Revolution*'s massive debt still hung over her head. She went back to work on the lecture circuit.

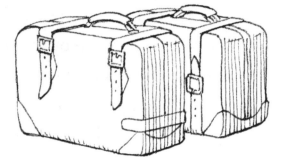

Chapter 8
New Frontiers

In 1876 the United States celebrated its one-hundred-year birthday. At the local celebrations in Philadelphia, Susan asked if the National could present a Declaration of Women's Rights. The organizers said no. The National did get a handful of tickets for members to sit on the platform. Susan listened to the Declaration of Independence being read.

Then she stood up and presented the women's
declaration to the pale, surprised man leading

the ceremonies. Anyone watching would
have thought it was part of the show.

The women even passed out copies to the crowd.

This was the second big victory for Susan that year. A few months earlier on May 1, 1876, she wrote in her diary "The day of Jubilee for me has come. I have paid the last dollar of the *Revolution* debt." She had paid ten thousand dollars plus interest nearly all by herself!

A month later, Susan was at Elizabeth's house

in Tenafly, New Jersey. They rummaged through old papers and newspaper clippings. The two friends couldn't believe how times had changed since they first started their fight. It was no longer shocking for women to speak in public. Women went to universities and worked at more jobs. Some women even had partial suffrage. They could vote in a few US territories and some local elections. Suffrage organizations existed across the country. More people joined every day in record numbers.

Many of the new women's rights activists were black, like the journalist Ida Wells who spoke out for the rights of women and all African Americans.

Susan and Elizabeth decided to write a book about the history of the suffrage movement. They threw themselves into the project. Elizabeth's daughter Hattie was called in to help. She was amazed at the way the two women worked.

Sometimes they would seem on the verge of
never speaking to each other again. Then they
would go for a walk arm-in-arm. Elizabeth said,
"Nothing that Susan could say or do could break
my friendship with her; and I know nothing could
uproot her affection for me."

IDA WELLS

IDA WELLS WAS BORN IN 1862 AS A SLAVE DURING THE CIVIL WAR. SHE WENT ON TO BECOME A JOURNALIST, NEWSPAPER EDITOR, SUFFRAGIST, AND—ALONG WITH HER HUSBAND, FERDINAND BARNETT—AN EARLY LEADER IN THE CIVIL RIGHTS MOVEMENT.

IN THE YEARS SINCE THE CIVIL WAR, BLACK WOMEN HAD STARTED TO DEMAND THEIR RIGHTS AS FREE CITIZENS. WOMEN'S SUFFRAGE HAD BECOME MORE A MORE POPULAR IDEA BUT, UNFORTUNATELY, EVEN IN THE WOMEN'S MOVEMENT MANY PEOPLE STILL OPPOSED RACIAL EQUALITY. IDA WELLS TRAVELED INTERNATIONALLY, SPEAKING OUT ON BEHALF OF EQUAL RIGHTS FOR WOMEN AND MEN OF ALL RACES.

Susan had always valued her friends. She valued them even more now that she had lost two of her sisters to tuberculosis—first Guelma and then Hannah. The women's movement had become like a family to her.

At fifty-seven, Susan was not as sprightly as she used to be. But she was still unstoppable and focused on her goal. From 1877 to 1883, she went from state to state to campaign for women's suffrage. She returned to Washington, DC, each year to speak to Congress. The first volume of Elizabeth and Susan's *History of Women Suffrage* was published in 1881.

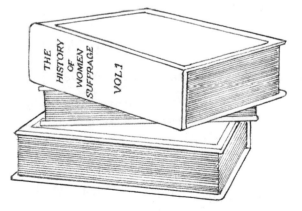

When the second volume was published a year later, Elizabeth went to Europe to promote the books. Susan had crisscrossed the continent

RACHEL AVERY

of North America many times, but she had never crossed the Atlantic Ocean. Susan decided to make the trip with Rachel Avery. Rachel was twenty-five and one of Susan's "nieces." The "nieces" were young women new to the movement who looked up to "Aunt Susan" as a role model and hero. Dozens of banquets and receptions and honors celebrated their departure for Europe. Susan and Rachel left America on the *British Prince* on February 23, 1883.

When the ship arrived in England, a friendly

face was waiting on the dock. Elizabeth "on the tiptoe of expectation" was there to meet her. "I came up to London the moment I heard of your arrival," she told Susan.

Susan stayed in Europe for nine months. During that time she helped form an International Council of Women where representatives from different countries could work together. She found that women in countries such as England, Ireland, Italy, Switzerland, and Germany were not so different from those in the United States. In November 1883 she set sail for home. She'd made many new friends, allies, and admirers abroad.

Chapter 9
Slow Progress

PRESIDENT GROVER CLEVELAND

In 1887, Congress voted for the first time on an amendment to the constitution that would give women the right to vote. The amendment didn't pass, but Susan didn't get discouraged. She hadn't expected it to pass. Just getting Congress to agree to vote on it had taken decades. Susan was busy making plans for the International Council of Women.

The conference took place from March 25

through April 1, 1888, in Washington, DC. Fifty-three organizations and forty-nine people from all over the world attended. President Grover Cleveland welcomed them to a reception at the White House. The council also marked another special occasion. For the first time in twenty years, the women of the American and the women of the National appeared together. Susan introduced her old rival Lucy Stone to make a speech. Other old friends included Frederick Douglass, who had first supported the women's movement way back in 1848.

Now the two major groups of the women's movement could work together. In 1890, when Susan was seventy, the National and American groups were joined together. Elizabeth was elected president of the new National American Woman Suffrage Association or NAWSA. Susan was vice president-at-large. After Elizabeth returned to Europe, Susan became the acting president.

Now that she was older, Susan thought about settling down. She had never owned a house of her own. In June 1891, she moved into her family home in Rochester. She and Mary would now live there together. Susan's "nieces" in the movement surprised her by decorating the house while she was out campaigning.

In 1895, activist Rachel Foster Avery surprised her with the gift of a retirement fund. All the "nieces" had contributed to it. Susan could now live comfortably for the rest of her life.

In 1896, California was set to vote on women's suffrage for their state. Susan campaigned hard, and it looked like they might win. But days before the election, the Liquor Dealers' League launched their own campaign 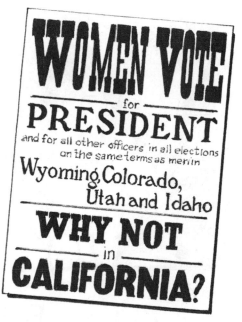 against the women. They convinced men that, if given the vote, women would immediately ban beer and whiskey. They even brought drunk men off the streets to vote!

California rejected women's suffrage.

But that very same year, Utah became a state with full women's suffrage, just as Wyoming, Colorado, and Idaho already had. Progress was slow, but Susan cherished every victory.

Chapter 10
Failure Is Impossible

As Susan approached her eightieth birthday, Carrie Chapman Catt was elected as the new NAWSA president. When the election results were announced, cheering filled the room. It was followed by a heavy silence at the thought that Susan B. Anthony was stepping down. Although she would never leave the group, an era had come to a close. Even Carrie Chapman Catt said, "Miss Anthony will never have a successor."

CARRIE
CHAPMAN CATT

The nineteenth century had also come
a close. In 1900, President McKinley
welcomed NAWSA to a reception at the
White House in Susan's honor. "Once I was
the most hated and reviled of women, now, it
seems as if everybody loves me," Susan said.

That fall in Rochester, Susan had a stroke. For a week, she couldn't speak at all. For a month, Mary cared for her constantly. Susan was never as strong as she had been before her stroke, but in June 1902, she went to visit Elizabeth. The two friends hugged when Susan was ready to go. She promised to return in November for Elizabeth's eighty-eighth birthday.

But a few months later, on a crisp fall day, Susan received a telegram from Elizabeth's daughter Hattie. It said simply: "Mother passed away at three o'clock." Susan sat silent for hours in her study, looking at Elizabeth's picture on the wall. When she stepped outside, reporters were waiting to hear what she had to say about the news. "I am too crushed to speak," Susan said.

Elizabeth's funeral was small, attended only by friends and family. When the casket was closed, a picture was placed on it, according to Elizabeth's wishes. It was a picture of her best friend, Susan B. Anthony.

Susan's doctors told her to get more rest, but she continued to travel. In 1903, she went to New Orleans. In 1904, she went to the International Council of Women in Berlin, Germany. In 1905, she travelled to Portland, Oregon.

Two weeks after the reelection of Theodore Roosevelt, Susan met with the president to ask for his help in finally giving women the vote. "Mr. Roosevelt," she said, leaning forward in her chair and grabbing his arm. "This is my principal request—it is almost the last request I shall ever make of anybody. Before you leave the presidential chair, recommend Congress to submit to the Legislatures a Constitutional amendment which will enfranchise women, and thus take your place in history with Lincoln, the great emancipator."

Roosevelt reminded her that he had spoken in favor of women's rights in the past. But he did nothing to help her cause now. He said congratulations when she turned eighty-six, but Susan was not impressed. "When will men do something besides extend congratulations?" she said. "I would rather President Roosevelt say one word to Congress in favor of amending the Constitution to give women suffrage than to praise me endlessly."

At the end of the evening of her birthday celebration, Susan was asked to say a few words. She stood beside activist Anna Shaw. Anna was now the president of NAWSA. Susan leaned on the younger woman's shoulder to stand. Susan began to speak about how women needed to carry on the struggle. Then, looking into the distance for a moment as if she could see the future, she announced, "Failure is impossible."

Those were the last words she ever spoke in public. She returned home to Rochester too weak to climb the stairs. She was helped to her bed. She was surrounded by her friends and her sister Mary.

One night Mary sat next to Susan. Anna Shaw sat at the foot of the bed. Susan began to speak the names of women she had known. Some Mary recognized as family. Some Anna knew as fellow suffragists. Some were people known only to Susan. "They all seemed to file past her dying eyes that day in an endless, shadowy review," Anna Shaw said later, "and as they went by she spoke to each of them."

Susan lay her cheek on Anna's hand. "I know how hard they have worked," she said. "I know the sacrifices they have made."

With that she closed her eyes. On Tuesday, March 13, 1906, Susan B. Anthony died.

She never lived to see women get the right

to vote. But the amendment she had fought so
hard for became law on August 18, 1920. It was
the Nineteenth Amendment to the Constitution.

But many simply called it the Susan B. Anthony Amendment.

Without her, it would never have happened.

TIMELINE OF
SUSAN B. ANTHONY'S LIFE

1820 —— Susan Brownell Anthony born in Adams, Massachusetts

1826 —— The Anthonys move to Battenkill, Massachusetts

1837 —— Daniel Anthony loses his mill in the financial
panic of 1837

1848 —— First Women's Convention held in Seneca Falls

1851 —— Susan meets Elizabeth Cady Stanton

1860 —— New York legislature passes act giving women
right to own property

1862 —— New York legislature repeals much of the law passed
in 1860
Susan's father dies

1863 —— Emancipation Proclamation frees slaves in southern states

1868 —— Fourteenth Amendment is ratified

1869 —— Territory of Wyoming grants women suffrage

1870 —— Territory of Utah grants women suffrage

1872 —— Susan B. Anthony arrested for voting

1880 —— Susan's mother dies

1883 —— Susan arrives in England

1902 —— Elizabeth Cady Stanton dies

1906 —— Susan B. Anthony dies

1920 —— Nineteenth Amendment is ratified, giving women
the right to vote

TIMELINE OF THE WORLD

Mary Wollstonecraft publishes *A Vindication of the Rights of Woman*	1792
Beethoven composes the Moonlight Sonata	1801
Napoleon defeated at the Battle of Waterloo	1815
Braille invented	1829
Charles Babbage invents the mechanical calculator	1835
Victoria becomes Queen of England	1837
Irish potato famine begins	1845
Publication of *Uncle Tom's Cabin* by Harriet Beecher Stowe	1852
Neanderthal fossil discovered and named in Germany	1856
The Civil War begins	1861
Publication of *Les Misérables* by Victor Hugo	1862
The ballet *Swan Lake* premieres	1877
Construction begins on the Eiffel Tower	1887
Jack the Ripper terrorizes London	1888
Publication of *The Interpretation of Dreams* by Sigmund Freud	1900
Finland becomes first European country to give women the vote	1906

BIBLIOGRAPHY

Barry, Kathleen. **Susan B. Anthony: A Biography of a Singular Feminist**. New York: New York University Press, 1988.

* Colman, Penny. **Elizabeth Cady Stanton and Susan B. Anthony: A Friendship That Changed the World**. New York: Henry Holt and Company, 2011.

Gurko, Miriam. **The Ladies of Seneca Falls: The Birth of the Woman's Rights Movement**. New York: Macmillan, 1974.

Lutz, Alma. **Susan B. Anthony: Rebel, Crusader, Humanitarian**. Washington, DC: Zenger Publishing Co. Inc., 1959.

Sherr, Lynn. **Failure Is Impossible: Susan B. Anthony In Her Own Words**. New York: Random House, 1995.

One Woman, One Vote. DVD. Produced by Ruth Pollak. 1995; Alexandria, VA: PBS Home Video, 2005.

Susan B. Anthony: Rebel for the Cause. DVD. Directed by Adam Friedman. 1995; New York: Biography A & E Home Video, 2005.

* Books for young readers